THE CALIFORNIA DUI HANDBOOK

THE BOOK POLICE DON'T WANT YOU TO READ

THE CALIFORNIA DUI HANDBOOK

THE BOOK POLICE DON'T WANT YOU TO READ

SCOTT D. HUGHES

WORD ASSOCIATION PUBLISHERS
www.wordassociation.com
1.800.827.7903

Published 2011.

Printed in the United States of America.

ISBN: 978-1-59571-696-5

Designed and published by

Word Association Publishers
205 Fifth Avenue
Tarentum, Pennsylvania 15084

www.wordassociation.com
1.800.827.7903

In This Book

INTRODUCTION

This book was written so that individuals arrested and charged with a DUI (driving under the influence of alcohol or drugs) in California will be able to understand the basic laws and defenses of a DUI charge. It is imperative that you have this information before you decide whether to exercise your right to consult with a lawyer and review the evidence presented against you. Whatever you do, do not make the mistake of pleading guilty before you know all of the facts.

Did you know that...

police in California arrest approximately 200,000 people every year for DUI and that 75% of all those arrested are convicted. Only a small fraction of those 150,000 who are convicted actually hire an attorney and an even smaller number, about 5%, go to trial. That means over a 100,000 people a year plead guilty to DUI charges without ever knowing what evidence the government has against them and without ever knowing whether that evidence is even admissible under the law.

Can you imagine a judge or jury *deciding* that you are guilty without ever hearing or seeing the evidence against you? Why then would you do that to yourself?

This happens because...

most people who go to court and just plead guilty do so because the police ***told*** them they were guilty. The police and the district attorneys count on people's ignorance of the law and their fear of harsher penalties, high legal fees, and public embarrassment without even questioning the charges against them.

The truth is...

the penalties for a DUI in California are getting more and more severe each year. By simply going to court and pleading guilty to a DUI, you face the following punishments:

- **Imprisonment and fine**
- **Probation**
- **License suspension**
- **Disallowance of restricted license**
- **Surrender of license**
- **Ignition interlock device** – a breathalyzer put in the steering column of your car, for which you must pay. Its purpose is to read your blood alcohol content, thereby preventing your car from starting unless your reading is below a certain level
- **Vehicle impound**
- **Restitution**
- **Participation in county alcohol and drug problem assessment program**
- **Penalty assessments, fees and state surcharge**

Whatever punishment you receive, the costs, both emotionally and financially, are great. Some people face actual job termination when their employer learns about their DUI conviction. A DUI conviction for those looking for work can destroy all chances of being hired, since most career applications require information about any previous convictions. Those who are convicted of an underage DUI must list it on their college applications and it could cost them acceptance. It should also be noted that an individual convicted of an underage DUI and caught failing to put it on their application is subject to immediate dismissal. For others, it's the embarrassment of family, friends and others in the community knowing of their arrest and conviction. The stigma could even affect their children, both psychologically and socially. Though the effects differ from person to person, the financial burden or the actual costs of a guilty plea without legal representation hit most people with equal force as fines, fees and court costs mount.

The state is counting on you to plead guilty without a fight because if even half of those arrested and charged with a DUI obtained an attorney and fought their charges, the entire court system in California would utterly collapse.

1

Clearing Up The Misconceptions About DUI

There are more misunderstandings, myths and misconceptions about DUI cases than almost any other legal matter. For example:

It is not true when people say that DUI cases cannot be won.

This belief leads people to plead guilty when they should have fought the weak evidence against them. Regardless of the circumstances in your particular case, if you have been accused of DUI, you have a constitutional right to the fairness, justice and protection that our legal system offers, including the presumption of innocence. You will learn as you read on that in many cases, evidence was gathered erroneously, samples taken were tainted or testing equipment was faulty. And these are just a few of the possible examples of defense arguments that can acquit you of a DUI charge.

It is not true that DUI cases are like every other criminal case.

DUI law is unlike most other laws. Some even believe that there is a DUI exception to the Constitution, which means that aspects of the laws regarding DUI do not recognize the individual's rights under the United States and California constitutions. A good example of this is a sobriety checkpoint where a police officer may temporarily detain you simply because you drove through it. Under other laws, an officer must have a sound reason for detaining you. DUI laws are, in many ways, complex, technical and vastly different from every other area of law.

It is not true that DUI is a minor offense.

Over the years, DUI laws have gotten tougher throughout the nation, while individuals remain ill–informed about the process and the rights they are guaranteed. Elected officials know they can win favor with voters by increasing the prosecutions and the severity of punishments for DUI. Some police departments even provide incentives for officers to make DUI arrests by recognizing and rewarding those with the most DUI convictions.

It is not true that all DUI cases are the same.

The consequences can be tragic if you assume that your case is just like any other DUI case. It's true that prosecutors must stick to a set mold to prove their cases, generally asking the same line of questions time and again. But, a good defense lawyer who is a specialist in defending DUI charges knows how to build a defense that is unique to your particular case. As a defendant, you should be represented by a lawyer who understands the individual and uncommon circumstances of your DUI case, which could and often do include some combination of law, science, medicine and physiology to varying degrees.

It is not true that any attorney can represent a person accused of DUI.

In the practice of law, it's impossible for one person to have the necessary training and experience to excel in all areas. You deserve the best representation possible and it could cost you dearly if you do not choose an attorney who is experienced and skilled in the complex area of DUI defense.

2

THE LESSON BEGINS WITH THIS FIRST AND FOREMOST...

Do not plead guilty to a DUI in California without being able to answer the following 10 questions:

1. What constitutes a DUI in California?
2. What happens to you when you are arrested for DUI?
3. What determines whether a detention, search or arrest is legal?
4. How can you be certain that chemical testing equipment was used following the manufacturers' requirements for fair and accurate testing?
5. Were the preliminary alcohol screening and evidentiary chemical testing devices properly maintained and calibrated prior to your testing?

6. Can the government prove that you were actually driving and that you were tested within three hours of driving?
7. Are the chemical test reports admissible?
8. Did the preliminary alcohol screening tests and/or the evidentiary chemical testing comply with Title 17 of the California Government Code?
9. Should you do your own independent analysis of the toxicology?
10. Do you have any other defenses?

1.What constitutes a DUI in California?

Under 21

If you are under 21 years of age, you are subject to California's Zero Tolerance Law. This means that if your blood alcohol content is 0.01% or greater, you will be charged with a DUI. A blood alcohol content of 0.05% or greater may result in you being charged with both an underage DUI as well as a regular DUI and you will most likely be arrested. Under such circumstances, a judge could confiscate your car. In all cases, you will have to pay thousands of dollars in fines, attend driving safety and alcohol/drug abuse classes, and submit proof of financial responsibility in order to have your license restored after suspension.

If you are under the age of 18 and convicted of DUI, you will lose your license for one year or until you reach the age of 18, whichever is greater. Underage drinkers should know that in order to reach a blood alcohol content of 0.01%, you need to only consume one 12–ounce beer, one four–ounce glass of wine or one 1.25–ounce of liquor. For some, these amounts will put a driver over 0.01%, often bringing them closer to 0.05%.

Over 21

If you are over 21 and arrested in California for a DUI, you will most likely be charged with two offenses – **California Vehicle Code Sections 23152(a) and 23152(b).**

California Vehicle Code Section 23152(a) states that it is a misdemeanor to drive a vehicle "while under the influence of any alcoholic beverage or drug, or under their combined influence."

If the DUI involves alcohol, under this section it is not necessary that the government prove any specific level of intoxication, though the government must prove you were *under the influence*, meaning your mental and motor skills were impaired. So, under this section, you can be guilty of a DUI if your blood alcohol or breath alcohol test results were less than 0.08% only if you were actually under the influence at the time of driving.

However, if your blood alcohol or breath alcohol level was less than 0.05%, it is presumed that you were not under the influence of alcohol. If the blood alcohol level was 0.05% or more, but less than 0.08%, there is no presumption either way. But, this fact may be considered with other competent (or admissible) evidence in determining whether the defendant was **not** under the influence.

If the DUI involves drugs, it is also not necessary that the government prove any specific degree of intoxication. However, the government must prove that you were **actually under the influence** of a drug at the time of driving.

California Vehicle Code Section 23152(b) states that "it is unlawful for any person who has 0.08% or more of alcohol in his or her blood to drive a vehicle."

Under this section, the government must prove that your specific level of intoxication is 0.08% or more. There is, however, no requirement for the government to actually prove you were under the influence if your breath alcohol or blood alcohol concentration was 0.08% or greater. For this reason, this statute is sometimes referred to as the "per se" DUI statute.

Specifically, this section states that there is a *rebuttable presumption* (an assumption made by a court that could be accepted unless someone contests it and proves otherwise) that you had 0.08% or more blood alcohol content at the time of driving the vehicle or 0.08% or more blood alcohol content at the time of the performance of a chemical test given within three hours after driving.

2. What happens to you when you are arrested for DUI?

Procedures vary depending on whether your criminal case is a felony or a misdemeanor. If you are charged with a first offense DUI, then most likely you are charged with a misdemeanor. A DUI is charged as a felony only when there is a collision with serious personal injury and/or property damage, or if it is your fourth DUI charge.

A misdemeanor DUI carries a maximum punishment of six months in jail and a $1,000 fine. Misdemeanor DUI cases are usually processed as follows:

1. Arrest
2. Arraignment
3. Pretrial
4. Jury Trial
5. Court Trial (almost never advisable)

Arrest

After you have been arrested for a misdemeanor DUI in California, the police must give you a temporary license. This license is as valid as your photo license card. The police may then release you on your own recognizance. If this happens, the police will give you a written notice to appear in court on a specific date and time for arraignment.

Arraignment

The arraignment is the first time you appear in court. The judge will call your case and you will have to stand while the judge reads the charges filed against you and formally advises you of your rights. If you are in custody, you must be arraigned within two court days of being arrested. If you are charged with a misdemeanor DUI, your attorney can most likely appear on your behalf without you being present. However, if you are charged with a felony, your presence will be required.

If you do not have an attorney and cannot afford one, you can request to apply for a public defender. Additionally, if you do not understand English, an interpreter will be provided.

There are three possible pleas you can make at the arraignment – guilty, not guilty and *nolo contendere* (no contest). A plea of guilty will end the case immediately and you will be sentenced. A plea of *nolo contendere* or no contest is the same as a guilty plea, except it cannot be used against you in a civil matter. A plea of not guilty will cause your case to proceed to the pretrial stage.

It is absolutely never advisable that you plead guilty at your arraignment without seeing the evidence in your case or discussing your case with a lawyer. This holds true even though the judge or prosecutor might attempt to get you to do so by threatening worse punishment should you not plead guilty. The other alternative is to continue the arraignment to a new date so that you can obtain your police report and complaint, then discuss your case with an attorney.

Pretrial

Prior to trial, the prosecution and the defense will have an opportunity to exchange information. This process is called *discovery.* During discovery, the defense attorney will be able to obtain all the records, reports, recordings, and maintenance and calibration logs that they need to best evaluate your case.

In addition, a defense attorney can file pretrial motions to set aside the complaint, dismiss the case or prevent evidence from being used at trial. Many times after filing these motions, the prosecution realizes that there may be a chance they could lose the case and, therefore, may negotiate a reduction of charges or penalties.

There may be several pretrial hearings before the actual trial in which the defense attorney will be given an opportunity to negotiate the case and obtain all the important discovery (evidence) needed to properly defend your case. Once sufficient information is obtained and analyzed, then and only then should your case be set for trial.

Jury Trial and Court Trial

The law establishes how much time should or should not elapse between arrest and trial in a criminal case. However, those time limits can be waived so that you or your lawyer can obtain discovery (evidence), hire an expert or launch an independent investigation of the facts of the case.

There are two types of trials – jury trials and court trials. A court trial is done without a jury, so the judge is both the judge and the jury. It is almost **never** advisable to elect to have a court trial. Because of this, I will discuss only the jury trial.

As I explained, before the trial begins your attorney will be able to argue which evidence may or may not be admissible during trial. Once these motions are heard and ruled upon, your attorney will then choose a jury. The process of selecting jurors from a large pool of potential jurors is called *voir dire.*

After the jury is selected, the trial begins with each side presenting opening statements. The prosecutors go first, presenting their side of the case. Then your lawyer will give the jury an overview of your version of what happened. In many ways, this can work in your favor because jurors are more likely to remember what they heard last.

During the trial, witnesses may testify and the lawyers will present evidence. Your lawyer may likely call upon an *expert* to testify in your behalf. Their testimony may focus on the chemical tests, the field sobriety tests, accident reconstruction or other scientific aspects of your case.

Once all the evidence is presented and the lawyers give their final arguments, with the prosecutors having the last word, the jury decides whether you are guilty or not guilty.

If the jury finds you ***not* guilty**, you will be free to leave and you can never be tried again for the same crime. If you are found ***guilty***, the case will be continued for sentencing at a later date. You may also choose to be sentenced right away.

If the jury cannot decide whether you are guilty or not guilty, this is called a hung jury. The judge will give additional instructions and encourage the jury to decide. But if they still cannot decide, the case will be declared a mistrial and you could be tried again. However, in a typical first offense DUI, the district attorney's office will most likely dismiss the case if the jury hangs.

Of course, if either side doesn't agree with the verdict, the misdemeanor can be appealed to the Appellate Department of the Superior Court.

3. What determines whether a detention, search or arrest is legal?

The Fourth Amendment to the United States Constitution provides that:

> The right of the people to be secure in their persons, houses, papers, and effects, against unreasonable searches and seizures, shall not be violated, and no Warrants shall issue, but upon probable cause, supported by Oath or affirmation, and particularly describing the place to be searched, and the persons or things to be seized.

You have the right to challenge the propriety of a search or seizure that violates your own reasonable expectations of privacy in the area searched or the items seized. A police officer in California may only arrest a person without a warrant:

a) whenever probable cause exists to believe the person has committed a felony; or
b) whenever probable cause exists to believe a misdemeanor has been committed in the officer's presence. California Penal Code Section 386; In re Thierry S., (1977) 19 Cal. 3d 727

Probable cause relates to evidence or facts in a case that would cause a reasonable person to believe that a crime or wrong–doing is being committed, has been committed or will be committed. Law enforcement officers must have probable cause before they can lawfully arrest a person for any crime. To determine if the police acted with probable cause in an arrest, the court will only look at the facts and circumstances presented to the officer at the time they were required to act and not on what information was found based on an illegal search or seizure.

The United States Supreme Court established the standards that police officers must follow when making a warrantless stop of a pedestrian in the case Terry v. Ohio, (1968) 392 U.S. 1. The burden is on the prosecution to show that the stop was based on specific, clearly–explained facts leading to a reasonable suspicion that criminal activity was afoot.

A police officer may only detain a citizen if the officer possesses: Specific and explainable facts causing them to suspect that (1) some activity relating to crime has taken place, is occurring or is about to occur, and (2) the person they intend to stop or detain is involved in that activity. Not only must they subjectively entertain such a suspicion, but it must be objectively reasonable for them to do so. The facts must be such as would cause any reasonable police officer in a similar position, drawing when appropriate on their training and experience, to suspect the same criminal activity and the same involvement by the person in question. In other words, an investigative stop or detention based on mere curiosity, rumor or hunch is unlawful, even though the officer may be acting in complete good faith.

Specifically in DUI cases, California courts have held that:

a) swerving alone may not be enough;
b) driving less than the speed limit is not enough unless it blocks traffic;
c) failing to signal prior to a lane change is not illegal unless it cannot be done safely, and
d) burning rubber is not enough.

California Vehicle Code Section 40300.5 provides that an officer may arrest a person only if the officer observes a violation of the law in their presence, or when the officer has reasonable cause to believe that the person had been driving while under the influence of an alcoholic beverage or any drug, or under the combined influence of an alcoholic beverage and any drug when any of the following exists:

a) the person is involved in a traffic accident;
b) the person is observed in or about a vehicle that is obstructing a roadway;
c) the person will not be apprehended unless immediately arrested;
d) the person may cause injury to themselves or damage property unless immediately arrested;
e) the person may destroy or conceal evidence of the crime unless immediately arrested.

The police officer's reports as well as the Department of Motor Vehicle (DMV) Form DS–367, page two, must provide a detailed description of the reason the officer pulled you over. It is very important that the reason(s) the officer gives be scrutinized to determine whether it is a valid, lawful reason.

Sobriety checkpoints

The California Supreme Court has held that sobriety checkpoints are lawful under the state and federal constitutions if they are conducted within certain limitations. The Court established the following guidelines for evaluating the intrusiveness of a sobriety checkpoint stop:

Guidelines for evaluating the intrusiveness of a sobriety checkpoint stop:

- Decisions to establish checkpoints and regarding site selection and procedures should be made by supervisors and not officers in the field.
- Decisions about which motorists are stopped should be made by applying a neutral formula and should not be at the officer's discretion.
- Primary consideration must be given to the safety of motorists and officers.
- The checkpoint must be at the most effective location to achieve the governmental interest, that is, on roads with high rates of alcohol–related accidents or arrests.
- Officers must exercise good judgment as to the time and duration of the checkpoints, considering effectiveness and safety.
- The checkpoint must appear to be duly authorized, with high visibility, warning signs, police vehicles and uniformed officers.
- The length of time each motorist is detained must be minimal. If the motorist does not display signs of impairment, they must be permitted to drive without further delay.
- If the officer observes signs of intoxication, the motorist may be directed to a separate area for field sobriety tests, at which point further investigation must be based on probable cause.

The United States Supreme Court further states that it is a violation of the Fourth Amendment for vehicle checkpoints to be established for the purpose of interdicting unlawful drugs because the primary purpose of the checkpoints was indistinguishable from the general interest in crime control. The Court noted that it supports brief, suspicionless seizures at a sobriety checkpoint only if they are aimed at removing drunk drivers from the road, but that it has never approved a checkpoint program whose *primary* purpose was to detect evidence of ordinary criminal wrongdoing. The fact that it may have a *secondary* purpose of keeping impaired motorists off the road does not make such a checkpoint constitutional.

If the officer violates your Fourth Amendment rights, all evidence found thereafter may not be used against you. Evidence seized as the result of an illegal search, seizure or arrest, or one which has exceeded permissible bounds is the "fruit of the poisonous tree" and must be excluded. However, this is not automatic. You must challenge the federal government and state that you did not consent to any search or detention by police and any such evidence obtained by police is in violation of your Fourth Amendment rights and protections, and should, therefore, be excluded.

If you, your home or your car is searched illegally, a judge might say that any evidence found during the search cannot be used against you in court. But if you or your lawyer does not object to the evidence before trial, the court might allow the evidence to be used.

4. How can you be certain that chemical testing equipment was used following the manufacturers' requirements for fair and accurate testing?

There are several ways to measure the level of alcohol in your body. The two most common ways that alcohol concentration is measured in California are breath and blood. Urine is rarely collected anymore, but could also be used.

Breath alcohol devices do not directly measure blood alcohol content or concentration, which requires the analysis of a blood sample. Instead, they estimate blood alcohol concentration indirectly by measuring the amount of alcohol in your breath, called deep lung alveolar.

Two breath–testing technologies are most prevalent. Desktop analyzers generally use infrared spectrophotometer technology, electrochemical fuel cell technology or a combination of the two. Hand–held field testing devices are generally based on electrochemical platinum fuel cell analysis and are used by police in the field as a form of a field sobriety test commonly called the Preliminary Alcohol Screening (PAS) test or as the evidential devices in Point of Arrest (POA) testing.

The accuracy of any breath or blood test certainly is dependant upon whether the devices or instruments were used consistently with the manufacturers' requirements. There are a number of different manufacturers of breath alcohol testing devices and blood alcohol testing devices that are approved by the National Highway Traffic Safety Administration for preliminary alcohol screening and for evidential tests. Each manufacturer has different requirements as to how these devices should be used. If the device is not properly used by law enforcement, this could alter the chemical testing results. For example, most breath test machines require operation between certain temperatures. Temperature is important, as the rate of the electrochemical reaction is affected by temperature. An elevated reading can occur if the device is not operated within the manufacturer's suggested operation temperature range.

Therefore, it is very important to know what devices were used in your case and to understand what the manufacturer's requirements are for accurately using each device. Following this, you must compare the manufacturer's requirements with how the officer actually used the device to determine if there are any discrepancies. This could not possibly occur if you show up at the arraignment without a lawyer and simply plead guilty because the officer said you are guilty.

Types of breath alcohol testing machines commonly used in California:

- Alcomat®
- ALERT® J4X
- Intoximeter® 3000
- Intoxilyzer® 5000 (64, 66, 68, EN)
- Draeger® 7410
- Draeger® 7110 MK–III
- Alco–Sensor® III
- Alco–Sensor® IV
- Intoximeter® ECIR
- Intoxilyzer® 8000

5. Were the preliminary alcohol screening and evidentiary chemical testing devices properly maintained and calibrated prior to your testing?

The police must meticulously maintain and re–calibrate their testing devices frequently to ensure any kind of accuracy. Calibration is the process of checking and adjusting the internal settings of a breath test device by comparing and adjusting its test results to a known alcohol standard.

Instrument calibration is one of the most fertile grounds for defense in a DUI case in California. The exact maintenance and calibration for the devices differ, obviously, for each type of device. However, there are standard minimum accuracy checks that must be performed with any device. In order to obtain accurate results, the device must be calibrated and properly maintained. There are many circumstances that can cause sensitivity to rise and, thereby, force high readings. Consistent accuracy checks might provide more confidence in the stability of the calibration, but these checks must be calibrated in the same environment in which they are used.

There are two methods of calibrating a precision fuel cell breath test device – the wet bath method and the dry gas method. In dry gas calibration, the device is tested using a mixture of alcohol and nitrogen. Wet bath calibration involves a mixture of alcohol and water. These procedures must be conducted by factory–trained technicians with the proper equipment. If the devices are not properly maintained and calibrated prior to testing, they could give false readings.

6. Can the government prove that you were actually driving and that you were tested within three hours of driving?

In a DUI case, the government must prove that you had 0.08% or more alcohol content in your breath or in your blood at the time of driving and that you had 0.08% or more alcohol content in your breath or blood at the time of the performance of a chemical test and that that test was administered within three hours after driving.

However, the three–hour time frame means nothing and **does not apply** if there is no evidence indicating the time you drove your vehicle. If the government cannot prove the time of driving, this presumption no longer applies and is rebutted. In addition, for the three–hour presumption to apply, the time of driving must be established by *competent* evidence, which is information that clearly proves a point and is then admissible evidence. But without this evidence, there is no *start time* from which to calculate three hours.

The time that you were driving can typically be proven by dispatch logs. When an officer makes a traffic stop, they transmit the information to dispatch, which then logs in that the officer has pulled you over, noting the start time. Most often, though, the police do not observe you actually driving your vehicle. In these situations, the government attempts to prove the time of driving from circumstantial evidence as opposed to direct evidence, which is more reliable. Therefore, circumstantial evidence may not be competent evidence to prove that you had been driving or the exact time you had been driving.

In order to prove that you had been driving, the police must eliminate every other possible driver. Once other possible drivers have been eliminated from consideration, your proximity to the vehicle is evidence from which a reasonable conclusion can be drawn that you were the driver. For example, if there is no evidence that you were the driver and there were other people at the scene who may have been driving, the government cannot prove that you had been driving nor can they prove the time that you had been driving.

What about parked vehicles?

The same issue arises in parked vehicle cases. California courts have held that arresting a person without a warrant is illegal when the person does not move their vehicle in an officer's presence, even if the person is seen by the officer sitting in the driver's seat of their lawfully–parked vehicle with the engine running.

7. Are the chemical test reports admissible?

Forensic Alcohol Reports are only admissible as *official records* if they are completed by the technician *at or near* the events in question. These reports clearly constitute hearsay, which is an out–of–court statement offered to prove the truth of the matter asserted. A common example of what constitutes *at or near* to qualify as an exception is a police DUI report, where the reports are typically prepared within an hour or two of the events related.

How late can a document be signed and still qualify for the hearsay exception?

The California Court of Appeals has held that a report prepared nearly a week after the forensic tests were completed does not fall within the statutory requirement that the report must be prepared *at or near* the time of the reported event.

A thorough review of the Forensic Alcohol Reports may lead to arguments which could result in the inadmissibility of the reports themselves due to their untrustworthiness of being prepared more than a week after the analysis was performed. Again, such a review cannot be completed if you plead guilty at arraignment without an attorney.

8. Did the preliminary alcohol screening tests and/or the evidentiary chemical testing comply with Title 17 of the California Government Code?

The California Government Code states the minimum requirements of testing and laboratory certification procedures. A review of the particular laboratory certifications as well as a detailed review of the testing procedures to determine whether they were done in compliance with Title 17 are very important in determining whether any of the chemical testing results are admissible evidence. If the toxicology results are inadmissible, the government has no case against you and most likely your charges will be dismissed.

Title 17 of the California Government Code requires strict compliance for admissibility of evidence. A breath sample may be collected only after you, the arrested person, have been under continuous observation for at least 15 minutes before its collection and during that time, you must not have ingested food or drink, smoked, regurgitated or vomited. 17 Cal Code Reg §1219.3. The arresting officer need not have direct and unbroken eye contact with you for this period, as long as the officer is able to use all of their senses to ensure compliance with the continuous observation requirement.

Title 17 requires that for each person tested, the breath alcohol analysis shall include analysis of two separate breath samples which do not differ from each other by more than 0.02 grams per 100 milliliters. 17 Cal Code Reg §1221.4.(a)(1).

Calibration must be done periodically. For the purposes of such determinations of accuracy, *periodic* means either a period of time not exceeding 10 days or following the testing of every 150 subjects, whichever comes first. Additionally, records must be kept of the testing of each machine. These records will need to be produced by the government in discovery.

Preliminary alcohol screening test results may only be admitted as substantive evidence (which is evidence that can verify the charges) of intoxication if they meet strict criteria. It must be clear that testing was administered in compliance with the forensic alcohol training and testing regulations contained in 17 Cal Code Reg §1221 et seq, or, alternatively, on proof of three foundational prerequisites: (1) the device was working properly, (2) the test was properly administered, and (3) the operator was competent and qualified.

In order to determine whether Title 17 has been strictly followed, extensive discovery needs to be obtained and reviewed. Therefore, it is very important to obtain this discovery very early in the case so that all of these issues can be analyzed.

9. Should you do your own independent analysis of the toxicology?

You have the right to have a sample – either blood or urine – retested by an independent laboratory. Your blood must be retained for one year after the date of collection and must be made available to you for additional testing. Upon motion of counsel, a judge routinely signs an order allowing you to have an independent lab take a sample of the blood or urine at the government lab and do an independent analysis at a private lab.

An independent analysis of the blood collected by the police at the time of the arrest may yield different results. For example, the government's lab may report your blood alcohol concentration as a 0.09%, yet an independent analysis might yield a 0.07% blood alcohol content, thus putting you below the legal limit. However, if your blood alcohol content is higher than 0.09%, it may be necessary to take a different approach to defending such a high percentage by examining:

1. How your blood was drawn
2. Whether blood samples were properly mixed
3. How samples were preserved
4. The possibility of fermentation
5. Whether the sample was properly refrigerated
6. The chain of custody
7. If analysis was done properly

It is important to keep in mind that the testing results are the strongest evidence that the government has against you. With this in mind, it is quite unreasonable to simply go to court and plead guilty without taking full advantage of the opportunity to review this evidence. It is vitally important that you know whether your blood was drawn properly by a licensed and certified phlebotomist, or whether the sample taken was properly mixed with the correct amounts of preservative, was properly refrigerated and handled, or whether the analysis was performed correctly. If you don't, you cannot possibly have an opinion as to whether you might be guilty or not guilty. The government or the police will not explain this to you. They expect that you will just plead guilty.

If you determine that an independent lab should obtain a sample of your blood and do its own analysis, you have to make the request from the court and obtain a court order.

10. Do you have any other defenses?

There are numerous possible defenses to a DUI that an experienced DUI attorney can explore. It takes a thorough discovery stage in order to obtain enough information to develop one of the arguments.

One of the most common causes of high alcohol readings on breath test results is actually caused from substances in the mouth when the test is supposed to be registering how much alcohol is in your lungs. But, residual alcohol in the mouth will result in a mistakenly high reading. For example, food trapped between the teeth can absorb alcohol and inflate the test readings. Even blood that is present in the mouth at the time the test is taken can skew the results. The breathalyzer cannot tell the difference between alcohol in the mouth (which is not a reliable indication of intoxication) from alcohol in the lungs (which is). Other substances in the mouth that can create an inaccurate test reading include:

- Mouth Alcohol (from sources such as breath sprays, mouthwashes and cold medication – see Table of Alternative Sources)
- Tongue Piercings and Dental Work
- Asthma Inhalers
- Food and *Alcohol–Free* beer (beer with an alcohol content of 0.5% or less)

Table Of Alternative Sources That May Increase The Alcohol Reading On A Breath Test

Brand Name (All items ™)	Manufacturer	Percent Alcohol(%)
Listerine Mouthwash	Warner–Lambert	26.9
Scope Mouthwash	Procter & Gamble	16.6
Nyquil	Richardson–Vicks	25.0
Benedryl Elixir Antihistamine	Parke–Davis	5.3
Cepacol.	Marion Merrell Dow	14.0
Sudafed Cough Syrup	Burroughs–Wellcome	2.4
Geritol Liquid	Smith Kline Beecham	12.0
Plax Mouthwash	Pfizer	7.5
ACT Mouthwash	Johnson & Johnson	7.0

Chemicals that can interfere with breath testing instruments:

- Aerosol sprays: Ethanol, isopropanol, toluene, xylene, nitrous oxide
- Antifreeze: Methanol, isopropanol
- Automotive/engine cleaning: Xylenes, ethylbenzene, tetrachloroethylene
- Degreasers: Isopropanol, n–butyl acetate, benzene, toluene, xylene, methylene
- Chloride
- Deodorizers: p–dichlorobenzene
- Drycleaning: 1,1,1–trichloroethane, tetrachloroethylene
- Gasoline: Benzene, toluene, xylene, naphthalene, n–hexane, n–heptane
- Glues: Toluene
- Lithography/printing supplies: Acetone, toluene, n–propanol methyl ethyl ketone, ethyl acetate
- Manicure supplies: Acetone, butylalcohol
- Model cement: Ethanol, isopropanol, acetone, toluene, xylene
- Nitrocellulose manufacturing: Ethyl acetate, butanol, n–butyl acetate, ethyl ether
- Paint thinner
- Methanol, ethanol, isopropanol, ethyl acetate, n–propyl acetate, acetone,
- methyl ethyl ketone, methyl butyl ketone, toluene, xylene, methylene
- Chloride, n–decane
- Cigarettes/smoking: Benzene, styrene
- Welding supplies: Acetylene, trichloroethane, acetone

Certain medical conditions may also create high breath test readings:

- Gastroesophageal Reflux Disease (GERD)
- Chronic Obstructive Pulmonary Disease (COPD)
- Diabetes

Breath test results can also be skewed if the officer administers the test less than 15 minutes after you have been belching, hiccupping or vomiting, as this increases the amount of alcohol on the breath.

3

GOING IT ALONE IS *NOT* WORTH THE GAMBLE

A DUI in California stays on your driving record and can be used against you for 10 years. Since being arrested for DUI can be a life–altering experience with serious financial, familial and social ramifications for years to come, it is never wise for you to go it alone and plead guilty just to get it over with.

Whether you are guilty or not guilty, it is your right to be represented by an experienced attorney. If you begin your research by looking in the phone book or online, you'll notice that almost every lawyer says the same thing. Everyone seems to offer a free consultation and most attorneys describe themselves as aggressive and experienced. What you need to know, however, is how to choose the right DUI lawyer for your particular case. We want you to make the best possible choice by knowing what questions you must ask. That way, you'll be able to retain the very best professional defense.

How many years have you been defending DUI cases?

It is vital that you choose someone who has real expertise in handling the complexities of DUI cases. Beware of the attorney who tries to convince you that DUI cases are like any other criminal cases. They definitely are not.

Are you a member of the National College for DUI Defense (NCDD)?

An attorney who is a member of NCDD is a specialist who has been accepted by a selective organization of attorneys committed to DUI advocacy.

How many cases have you taken to jury trial?

If your case must go to trial in order for you to get the best possible outcome, it is crucial that you hire an attorney who has a significant amount of jury trial experience.

Have you won DUI cases?

Even though past successes do not guarantee any particular outcome in your case, you should know whether or not this lawyer has had successful defenses.

Where can I read about your other cases?

Lawyers should be able to share with you either copies of transcripts or opinions without revealing the names of former clients.

What are my potential legal costs, including investigators and experts?

An attorney should be able to give you clear and honest figures. Beware of anyone who promises low costs and fees.

What possible problems do you see in my case?

It is your right to know what obstacles the lawyer sees that could affect the final resolution of your case. And while no reputable lawyer can possibly promise a specific result, it is important that you are certain that this lawyer recognizes the challenges that are specific to your case.

As a potential client, it is important that you understand how a lawyer runs their office and their practice. Here are some questions that should help you decide if a prospective attorney is someone you want working for you.

- Do you routinely put your fee arrangements in writing?
- Can I see a written fee arrangement?
- Do you accept credit cards?
- Do you accept payments?
- Do you have a toll free number?
- Do you return telephone calls the same day that you receive them?
- How often do you check your email?
- Do you answer emails the same day that you receive them?
- If you are not available, do you have administrative assistants who can give me basic information about my case?

Following your initial meeting with an attorney and before you make your decision, ask yourself:

- Did this lawyer listen to me?
- Did this lawyer carefully inquire about the events preceding my arrest and charge, including the reason given by the officer for stopping me?
- Did this lawyer ask me to detail all statements made by the officer, all statements I may have made to the officer and the conditions upon which those statements were made?
- Did this lawyer ask for a detailed description of the area where I may have been tested.
- Did this lawyer ask me about the names and contact information of any potential witnesses.
- Did this lawyer inquire about the results of all of my tests?
- Did this lawyer speak in a way that I could understand?
- Did this lawyer welcome all of my questions?
- Did this lawyer answer all of my questions to my satisfaction?
- Did this lawyer seem defensive or avoid answering any of my questions?

Since every case is different, you may have many other questions that are important to you. The answers that you receive from each lawyer you interview will make all the difference to you and your family. Your decision to hire a DUI lawyer may be the most important decision you make this year. Much hangs in the balance for you and your family.

4

Your Experience With The Law Offices Of Scott D. Hughes

Over the years, I have learned that I cannot and should not accept every case. The type of case preparation that I do and the level of communication that I feel is necessary takes a great deal of time. Therefore, a smaller client load affords me the time to fully process the details of your case and be certain that you understand your situation, your options and the best way to proceed.

When you meet with me or call me to ask those questions that I believe are vital for a prospective client have an attorney answer, the following is what I will tell you:

Do you routinely put your fee arrangements in writing?

Yes we do. Our written agreement will spell out in plain English our obligations to you. You will be given a copy of the agreement for your records.

Can I see a written fee arrangement?

You will be given a written fee arrangement at our in–itial consultation.

Do you accept credit cards?

Yes, we accept payment by all credit cards and PayPal.

Do you accept payments?

We do accept payments and will negotiate terms during your initial consultation.

Do you have a toll free number?

Our toll free number is 1–888–398–0564. We are available 24 hours a day, seven days a week.

Do you return telephone calls the same day that you receive them?

My office takes great pride in the fact that we respond to phone calls the same day they are received.

How often do you check your email?

We check email constantly throughout the course of the day.

Do you answer emails the same day that you receive them?

Again, our office takes great pride in the fact that we respond to emails the same day they are received.

If you are not available, do you have administrative assistants who can give me basic information about my case?

Certainly. Anyone on my staff is able to provide you with basic information about your case.

Once you have made your decision, it all begins with an intake interview (a sample follows on the next two pages). The intake interview gives me an immediate overview of the details of your case so that I can plan a successful course of action.

Sample intake interview

LAW OFFICES OF SCOTT D. HUGHES
A PROFESSIONAL LAW CORPORATION
620 NEWPORT CENTER DRIVE, SUITE 1100 · NEWPORT BEACH, CA 92660
TELE. (714) 423-6928 · FAX. (714) 845-0030
WWW.SCOTTHUGHESLAW.COM

TO: **FILE**

FROM: **SDH**

RE: **DUI INTAKE INTERVIEW**

DATE:

INTAKE INTERVIEW OF ______________________
(XXX) XXX-XXXX

Date/Time of Arrest:
Location of Arrest:

Date/Time of Court:
Location of Court

Date/Time of DMV:
Location of DMV:

Client Profile:

Daily Activity:

DUI Stop:

FST:

Weather:
Surface:
Lighting:
Dress:
Shoes:
Video:
Audio:
Officer:
Distractions:
Notes:
Tests:

Walk and Turn:
One Leg Stand:

PAS:

Arrest:

City Jail:

Blood/Breath:

Booking and Release:

Medicals

Age
Height
Weight

Head Trauma

Doctor

Meds

Allergies

Head

Eyes

Larynx

Globus

Stomach

Hearing

Dental

Surgery

Speech

Physical

My experience as a DUI lawyer can greatly increase your chances of winning your case. This is true not only for first time offenders, but also in the cases of second, third and fourth time offenders.

5

Life After Your DUI– What Every Driver Should Know

Being Pulled Over – *Again*

Your first arrest for DUI should serve to educate you about your future conduct behind the wheel. Therefore, it is our wish that your first DUI arrest will be your only DUI arrest. Whether you were guilty or not guilty of the charges, it is, of course, of vital importance that you never again endanger the lives of others or yourself by driving while under the influence of alcohol or drugs. But if you plead guilty to first–time charges or even if you plead not guilty but are found guilty, the penalties for future subsequent DUI arrests should definitely give you pause and a compelling reason to never again drive while under the influence.

In California, a first drunk driving conviction can result in 96 hours to six months in jail, a fine from $1,000 to $1,600, a six–month license suspension and other penalties. A second offense, however, calls for 90 days to one year in jail, a fine from $1,000 to $1,900, a license suspension for two years and other penalties. As you might expect, third and fourth offenses increase the sentence exponentially. Furthermore, a new California law, Assembly Bill 1165, makes it unlawful for a person who is on probation for a DUI offense to operate a motor vehicle at any time with a blood alcohol concentration of 0.01% or greater.

If you are that person who has been convicted of a first–time DUI offense and a police officer suspects that you were driving under the influence and pulls you over, here are some things that you need to know. First, the officer must have had a reasonable suspicion before they pulled you over. The most common are:

- Driving on or over the lane divide
- Drifting into the other lane
- Making a wide turn
- Making an illegal turn
- Weaving in your lane
- Breaking frequently
- Nearly missing an object or another car
- Driving very slowly, generally more than 10 miles per hour below the speed limit
- Swerving
- Driving with headlights off
- Not using turn signals or making inappropriate turn signals
- Stopping in the middle of the road for no reason
- Accelerating or decelerating too quickly
- Following another car too closely

None of these infractions necessarily mean that you were driving under the influence. But if you are charged with a DUI, it can be immensely helpful if you are able to provide a non–alcohol related explanation for your driving. Since what you say when stopped by a police officer later goes into the written report, it is always imperative that you be respectful and cooperative, even if you feel the officer is wrong or unfair. It is best that you speak only when spoken to and do so to provide the officer with what is requested. You will first be asked to show your driver's license, registration and proof of insurance. If you fail to do so promptly, it is legal for the officer to search your vehicle in any location within the passenger compartment where it is reasonable to store a driver's license or vehicle registration.

If the officer suspects that you were driving while intoxicated, they will be looking for a number of traditional indicators of intoxication, including:

- Odor of alcohol
- Bloodshot or watery eyes
- Slurred speech
- Flushed face complexion
- Lack of coordination such as fumbling to find your license

You will likely be asked if you have consumed any alcoholic beverages and it is perfectly within your legal rights to respectfully refuse to answer. The officer may still arrest you, but refusing to answer the question is not reason enough to be arrested. However, if you have truly not had anything to drink, it is best to say so.

If the officer asks you to get out of the car, refusal to do so is grounds for arrest. The same is true if the officer attempts to pat you down. You have a right to refuse to allow the officer to search your vehicle. Be advised, however, that in some limited cases when the officer has probable cause, your car may be searched without your permission. It is important to remember, however, that even if you believe that what the officer is doing is illegal, **do not resist**. If the officer illegally obtains evidence against you, it cannot be used at trial.

The officer may administer a field sobriety test and you do have a legal right to refuse. The best way to refuse, however, is to politely say that you would prefer to speak to an attorney before taking the test.

If you do take the test, the officer will examine your eyes for watering and to determine whether they can smoothly track and follow a finger or a pencil 12 to 15 inches from your nose. The officer will also measure your balance while your mental attention is focused on something else. You will be asked to walk a specified number of heel–to–toe steps away, then turn and walk the same number back. You will fail this part of the test if you begin too early, step off the line, lose your balance, lose count of how many steps you took, put space between your heel and to toe, or use your arms for balance. The officer will also ask you to close your eyes, extend your arms and touch you finger to your nose. You will fail this part of the test if you begin too early, have trouble maintaining your balance, miss your nose or show any sign of muscle tremors. Finally, you will be told to stand erect, close your eyes, tilt your head back and estimate how long thirty seconds lasts.

Who decides whether you pass or fail? It is the officer. Now do you see why it's best to be respectful and cooperative? These tests are entirely subjective and do not conclusively determine whether you are drunk or not. It is interesting to note that most people do not pass these tests, even if they had not been drinking. An uneven pavement, the volume of nearby traffic, your nerves and fear, the amount of lighting available, the temperature and weather conditions, the type of shoes you are wearing – all of these and more can affect the outcome of the test.

Finally, no matter how you did on the field test – and I will repeat that most people don't do well – an experienced defense attorney will tell you that these results alone will not convict you. The operative phrase, however, is an experienced attorney. Whether it is your first offense, second, or third, it is a dangerous idea to go it alone.

Conclusion

Despite your age, situation, circumstances, previous offense, or even your guilt or innocence, it cannot be emphasized enough that when you are charged with a DUI, you need legal representation. The state of California has a prosecuting attorney who will be launching a vigorous case against you. The police will be providing the prosecutor with evidence to be used against you, which may or may not be accurate or even legal. Why would you not make every effort to defend yourself with a professional who knows and understands the system. The law is complicated and it can be difficult for you to be certain that your rights are being protected.

Even though I have written this book to educate and inform, there are simply too many ways in which an individual can be wrongly arrested and convicted. Don't let that happen to you.

About The Author

Scott D. Hughes served his country as a Military Police Officer in the United States Marine Corps. There he received a Good Conduct Medal and numerous Letters of Accommodation and Meritorious Masts.

Mr. Hughes attended the prestigious State University of New York at Albany (SUNY) for Criminology and obtained a Bachelor's Degree in both Criminal Justice and English Literature. He completed his Master's Degree from SUNY in one year and graduated Cum Laude.

In 2007, he graduated with *Honors* from Western State University College of Law, where he was Managing Editor of the Western State Law Review in 2005 and Assistant Managing Editor in 2006. Upon passing the California Bar Examination, Mr. Hughes has practiced law in the areas of DUI and Criminal Defense. He regularly practices before courts in Orange County and Los Angeles County and throughout all of Southern California.

WA

Made in the USA
Monee, IL
04 November 2026

67381818R10036